# BECOME A BRILLIANT
# VISION EXECUTIVE

Go Beyond the Spark

**LILLIAN OYELEYE**

# BECOME A BRILLIANT VISION EXECUTIVE

*Go Beyond the Spark*

By

**Lillian Oyeleye**

**Become a Brilliant Vision Executive:** Go Beyond the Spark by Author Lillian Oyeleye © March 2024. Published by Prestige Editors. Read more about Prestige Editors [here](here).

**To contact the publisher**

contact.prestigeeditors@gmail.com
(+234) 09050749803
Ile-Ife, Nigeria

**Book Serial Number (BSN)**
BBCO/090324

**All Rights Reserved**

No part of this book may be produced, or stored in a retrieval or transmitted in any form or by any means, electronic, mechanical, photocopying, recording, or otherwise, without the written permission of the author/publisher.

For any use that may violate our Copyright, please contact the publisher, Prestige Editors with the details above.

# Table of Contents

| | |
|---|---|
| Dedication | 5 |
| Introduction | 5 |
| CHAPTER 1 | 10 |
|     **Vision Ignition** | |
| CHAPTER 2 | 15 |
| **Mindset for Brillance** | |
| CHAPTER 3 | 19 |
| **Vision Crafting and Storytelling** | |
| CHAPTER 4 | 24 |
| **Building Your Dream Team** | |
| CHAPTER 5 | 29 |
| **Strategic Execution** | |
| CHAPTER 6 | 33 |
| **Innovation and Growth-Hacking** | |
| CHAPTER 7 | 37 |
| **The Place of Purpose and Legacy** | |
| APPENDIX A | 41 |
| **OTHER BOOKS BY THE SAME AUTHOR** | |
| APPENDIX B | 41 |
| **CONNECT WITH US** | |

## Dedication

This book is dedicated to all the visionary individuals striving to bring something extraordinary into existence. I understand the challenges and uncertainties you face on this journey, but I urge you to persevere and keep pushing, you are almost there.

## Introduction

Have you ever felt like your career is a bland, pre-packaged meal – lacking flavor, sustenance, and the promise of something truly satisfying? Many professionals find themselves navigating their careers on autopilot, drifting from role to role without a clear sense of direction. The result? A gnawing feeling of unfulfillment and a yearning for a more flavorful professional experience.

This book is your invitation to a different kind of culinary adventure – one where you craft the recipe for a fulfilling career journey. Forget the pre-packaged options; here, you'll discover the ingredients to ignite your vision, a powerful force that propels you towards a career rich in meaning, purpose, and impact.

Think of yourself as a brilliant visionary chef, meticulously selecting the ingredients that will define your professional signature dish. This book serves as your essential culinary guide, equipping you with the tools and strategies to:

- **Uncover your purpose:** The underlying "why" that fuels your passion and shapes your career aspirations.
- **Spark your big idea:** The unique blend of skills, talents, and experiences that make your professional vision truly your own.
- **Craft your guiding vision:** A concise yet powerful statement that encapsulates your aspirations, values, and the impact you want to make.

Throughout this book, we'll delve into the essential elements of this culinary career creation process. We'll explore strategies for building a strong network – your "dream team" – of mentors and collaborators. We'll hone your strategic execution skills, ensuring your vision translates into tangible reality. Most importantly, we'll cultivate the growth mindset – the belief that your skills and abilities can be cultivated through effort and learning – a key ingredient for a career journey that remains fresh and adaptable in today's dynamic professional landscape.

**So, are you ready to ignite your vision and embark on a career journey that's as delicious as it is impactful? Let's GO!**

**LILLIAN OYELEYE**

# CHAPTER 1

# Vision Ignition

At a critical juncture in your career, the path ahead can feel like an endless maze. Every turn offers a new direction, but without a clear vision, you're left to navigate blindly. This is the reality for many professionals who find themselves in a cycle of unfulfilling roles, their talents underutilized and their passion dormant.

The antidote? **Vision ignition.** It's a process of self-discovery that ignites your passion and propels you towards a meaningful career journey. Think of it as the strategic foundation for your professional life. Just as a successful entrepreneur meticulously selects resources, leverages strengths, and refines their approach, you too can curate your ideal career vision. This chapter serves as your strategic guide, equipping you with the tools to discover your purpose, spark your big idea, and define your guiding vision.

**The foundational step – uncovering your purpose.** Purpose transcends mere professional goals; it's the underlying "why" that fuels your motivation and shapes your career aspirations. Ask yourself: What intrinsic values do I yearn to express through my work? Does intellectual stimulation energize me, or am I driven by a desire to contribute to a social impact? Perhaps you crave the challenge of building something from the ground up, or find immense satisfaction in mentoring and guiding others. Understanding your purpose is the core principle in your career strategy, imbuing it with meaning and direction.

**For instance, consider Sarah, a brilliant marketing professional.** While Sarah excelled at crafting compelling campaigns, a nagging feeling persisted. Through introspection, Sarah realized her true passion lay in empowering others. She craved a role where she could mentor young marketers and help them unlock their full potential. This newfound understanding of her purpose ignited a spark, propelling her to explore career paths in leadership development or educational marketing.

**Once you've identified your purpose, it's time to ignite the spark of your big idea.** This is where your unique skills, passions, and experiences come into play. Reflect on past projects that ignited your enthusiasm. What aspects of those roles resonated most deeply with you? What skills did you excel at, and what challenges did you find invigorating? By analyzing your past successes and interests, you begin to identify the unique components that will make up your signature career strategy.

**Take David, for example.** Throughout his career, David thrived in fast-paced environments where innovation was encouraged. His analytical mind and problem-solving skills were his greatest assets. By recognizing these strengths and his passion for cutting-edge technology, David formulated a vision to become a leader in the field of artificial intelligence.

**Finally, with purpose and potential components in hand, it's time to define your guiding vision.** This vision serves as the roadmap for your professional journey. It's a concise statement that encapsulates your aspirations, values, and the impact you want to make. Your vision should be audacious enough to inspire you yet specific enough to guide your decision-making.

Throughout the following chapters, we'll delve deeper into the strategic art of career crafting. We'll explore strategies for building a strong network of mentors and collaborators, hone your strategic execution skills, and embrace continuous learning to ensure your vision remains fresh and relevant.

**Remember, a fulfilling career isn't a pre-packaged template – it's a masterpiece you create yourself.** By embarking on this journey of vision ignition, you'll discover the components that make your professional journey uniquely impactful and aligned with your core values.

# CHAPTER 2

# Mindset for Brillance

The seeds of a successful career vision are sown in fertile ground – the ground of your mindset. Just as a thriving garden requires specific conditions for growth, so too does your professional journey depend on cultivating a set of core mental attitudes. This chapter delves into the essential ingredients for a **mindset of brilliance**, focusing on the development of confidence, resilience, and the coveted growth mindset.

**Confidence is the cornerstone of a brilliant vision.** It's the unwavering belief in your abilities and the potential of your vision. It empowers you to navigate challenges, seize opportunities, and inspire those around you. Building confidence is an ongoing process, fueled by self-awareness and a willingness to step outside your comfort zone. Celebrate your past successes, both big and small. Seek opportunities to learn and grow, even from setbacks. Over time, with each accomplishment and conquered fear, your confidence will solidify, becoming the bedrock of your vision.

**Resilience, the unwavering spirit in the face of adversity, is equally crucial.** The path to achieving your vision will inevitably be strewn with obstacles. Unexpected setbacks, challenging colleagues, and moments of self-doubt are all part of the journey. However, a brilliant visionary isn't deterred by these hurdles. They possess the resilience to bounce back, learn from setbacks, and emerge stronger. Develop your resilience by acknowledging challenges head-on, seeking support from your network, and maintaining a positive outlook. Remember, every obstacle overcome strengthens your resolve and fuels your passion.

**Finally, the growth mindset is the secret weapon of brilliant visionaries.** It's the belief that your skills and abilities can be cultivated through effort and learning. Those with a growth mindset view challenges as opportunities to learn and grow, setbacks as stepping stones, and failure as a chance to refine their approach. This mindset fosters continuous improvement, keeping your vision fresh and adaptable in a dynamic professional landscape. Embrace the growth mindset by stepping outside your comfort zone, seeking out new challenges, and celebrating the learning process as much as the achievements.

By cultivating a mindset that blends unwavering confidence with the resilience to weather any storm and the growth mindset to continuously evolve, you empower yourself to become a brilliant leader and visionary.

# CHAPTER 3

# Vision Crafting and Storytelling

A powerful vision isn't merely an aspiration; it's a compelling narrative that ignites action and inspires others. Just as a captivating story draws us in and holds our attention, your vision statement, when crafted effectively, can become a rallying cry for your career journey.

This chapter delves into the **art of vision storytelling**, equipping you with the strategies to translate your vision into a narrative that resonates and inspires. Effective storytelling hinges on a few key elements:

**Clarity and Concision:** Your vision statement should be a clear and concise encapsulation of your aspirations. Avoid jargon and ambiguity. Imagine yourself explaining your vision in an elevator pitch – you want to capture your essence in a few impactful sentences.

**Passion and Purpose:** Infuse your vision statement with the passion that fuels your journey. What excites you about your vision? What impact do you hope to achieve? By injecting your enthusiasm, you make your vision more relatable and inspiring.

**Specificity and Action:** While your vision should be audacious, it also needs to be specific enough to guide your actions. Instead of simply stating a desire for "success," consider outlining the specific impact you want to make or the legacy you want to leave. This specificity provides direction for your career path and decision-making.

**Here's an example to illustrate these principles:**

**Generic Vision:** "To be a successful leader in the technology industry."

**Compelling Vision Narrative:** "By leveraging my expertise in artificial intelligence, I aim to revolutionize the healthcare industry, developing innovative solutions that improve patient outcomes and democratize access to healthcare on a global scale."

The first statement lacks detail and passion. The second, however, paints a clear picture of the individual's aspirations, their area of expertise, the desired impact, and the global reach of their vision.

**Storytelling doesn't stop at your vision statement.** Throughout your career journey, you'll have opportunities to share your vision with others – potential employers, colleagues, and collaborators. Utilize storytelling techniques to capture their attention and garner support. Use vivid language, compelling anecdotes, and a touch of vulnerability to connect with your audience on a deeper level.

**By mastering the art of vision storytelling, you transform your vision from a personal ambition to a powerful narrative that inspires action and empowers you to achieve extraordinary things.** In the next chapter, we'll explore the importance of building a strong network – your "dream team" – to support you on your journey.

# CHAPTER 4

# Building Your Dream Team

The path to achieving a brilliant vision is rarely a solitary trek. Just as a successful entrepreneur leverages the strengths of a skilled team, so too do brilliant visionaries surround themselves with a powerful network – their "dream team." This dream team isn't merely a collection of colleagues; it's a strategic network of mentors, collaborators, and supporters who empower you to achieve extraordinary things.

**Building your dream team starts with attracting the right people.** Identify individuals who complement your skillset and share your core values. Seek out mentors who possess the experience and wisdom to guide you through challenges. Look for collaborators who bring diverse perspectives and expertise to the table.

**Effective communication is the cornerstone of a strong dream team.** Clearly articulate your vision, goals, and expectations to your network. Actively listen to their insights and perspectives. Foster an environment of open communication and trust, where collaboration thrives.

**Here are some practical strategies to cultivate your dream team:**

- **Leverage your existing network:** Reconnect with former colleagues, classmates, and professional acquaintances. You'd be surprised at the hidden gems you might discover within your existing network.
- **Seek out industry events and conferences:** Attend industry gatherings and conferences to connect with like-minded individuals and potential mentors.

- **Utilize online platforms:** Professional networking platforms like LinkedIn can be a powerful tool for connecting with others in your field.
- **Offer value in return:** Building a strong network is a two-way street. Be willing to offer your expertise, mentorship, or support to others in your network.

**The power of collaboration shouldn't be underestimated.** By surrounding yourself with a diverse and supportive team, you gain access to a wider range of knowledge, perspectives, and resources. This collective intelligence amplifies your vision's potential and empowers you to navigate challenges with greater agility.

**Think of your dream team as a synergistic force multiplier.** Each member brings their unique strengths and experiences to the table, creating a collective impact far greater than the sum of its parts. Through open communication, trust, and a shared vision, your dream team becomes the wind beneath your wings, propelling you towards achieving your professional aspirations.

# CHAPTER 5

# Strategic Execution

A powerful vision is the compass that guides your career journey. However, a compass alone doesn't ensure you reach your destination. The process of translating your vision into reality requires the art of **strategic execution**. This chapter equips you with the tools to set actionable goals, manage resources effectively, and navigate challenges with agility.

**Strategic execution begins with the creation of a roadmap.** Break down your vision into achievable milestones, setting SMART goals (Specific, Measurable, Achievable, Relevant, and Time-bound) for each stage of your journey. These goals provide a clear path forward, keeping you focused and motivated.

**Effective resource management is paramount.** Identify the resources required to achieve your goals, whether it's time, talent, financial capital, or access to specific technologies. Utilize your network and negotiation skills to secure the resources necessary to fuel your vision's progress.

**Challenges are inevitable on the path to achieving a brilliant vision.** The key lies not in avoiding them, but in developing the agility to navigate them effectively. Anticipate potential roadblocks, and formulate contingency plans to address them. When setbacks occur, maintain a positive outlook, learn from the experience, and adapt your approach as needed.

Here are some key strategies for navigating challenges with agility:

- **Embrace a growth mindset:** View challenges as opportunities to learn and improve. This perspective fosters resilience and fuels your determination to overcome obstacles.

- **Seek diverse perspectives:** When faced with a roadblock, tap into your network for support and alternative solutions. The collective wisdom of your dream team can be invaluable in navigating complex challenges.
- **Maintain a focus on your vision:** During moments of difficulty, remember the "why" behind your vision. Reconnecting with your core purpose can reignite your passion and guide you through challenging times.

**Strategic execution is an ongoing process, a continuous cycle of planning, action, evaluation, and adaptation.** Regularly assess your progress, identify areas for improvement, and refine your approach as needed. Embrace a data-driven approach, utilizing metrics and feedback to ensure your strategies remain relevant and effective.

# CHAPTER 6

# Innovation and Growth-Hacking

In today's dynamic business landscape, stagnation is the enemy of progress. Brilliant visionaries understand the importance of **perpetual innovation**, fostering a culture of creativity and embracing new technologies to continuously evolve and amplify their vision's impact. This chapter explores strategies for "growth hacking" – unconventional and data-driven approaches to accelerate your professional growth and achieve remarkable results.

**At the heart of innovation lies a culture of creativity.** Encourage open communication within your dream team, where diverse perspectives and ideas are valued. Embrace experimentation, allowing room for calculated risks and fostering a "fail-fast, learn faster" mentality.

**Technology is a powerful catalyst for innovation.** Stay informed about emerging trends in your field and explore how new technologies can enhance your vision. Whether it's leveraging artificial intelligence to streamline processes or utilizing data analytics to gain deeper customer insights, embrace technology as a tool to propel you forward.

**Growth hacking is a strategic approach to maximizing your vision's impact.** It focuses on utilizing unconventional, data-driven methods to achieve exponential growth. This could involve identifying low-cost, high-impact marketing strategies or streamlining processes to improve efficiency.

Here are some key principles of growth hacking:

- **Focus on data-driven decision making:** Collect and analyze data to identify areas for improvement and measure the effectiveness of your strategies. Data empowers you to make informed decisions and adapt your approach in real-time.
- **Embrace experimentation:** Don't be afraid to experiment with new ideas and

approaches. Test your assumptions, track results, and iterate based on your findings.
- **Think outside the box:** Challenge the status quo and explore unconventional solutions. Sometimes, the most effective strategies are the ones that haven't been attempted before.

**By fostering a culture of creativity, embracing new technologies, and adopting a growth hacking mindset, you equip yourself to continuously refine and scale your vision.** This adaptability ensures your vision remains relevant and impactful in a rapidly evolving professional landscape.

**Remember, innovation is not a one-time event; it's a continuous journey.** By nurturing a culture of exploration and experimentation, you empower yourself and your dream team to achieve remarkable things. The final chapter of this book will delve into the importance of legacy and maintaining of purpose, even in the face of adversity.

# CHAPTER 7

# The Place of Purpose and Legacy

A truly brilliant vision transcends personal ambition. It has the power to create a ripple effect, leaving a lasting positive impact on the world around you. This chapter explores the importance of **leading with purpose** and embracing **social responsibility**, ensuring your career journey contributes to a greater good.

**Leadership is not about titles or positions; it's about inspiring others to achieve extraordinary things.** As you navigate your career path, strive to be a leader who motivates and empowers those around you. Foster a collaborative environment where diverse perspectives are valued and individual strengths are amplified. Lead with integrity and a commitment to ethical practices, setting a positive example for others.

**Social responsibility is the cornerstone of a legacy-driven career.** Brilliant visionaries understand the interconnectedness of business and society. They actively seek opportunities to contribute to positive social change, whether it's promoting environmental sustainability, fostering diversity and inclusion, or supporting charitable causes aligned with their values.

Here are some ways to integrate social responsibility into your vision:

- **Champion diversity and inclusion:** Foster a work environment that celebrates diverse perspectives and backgrounds. By leveraging the collective wisdom of your team, you create a more innovative and successful enterprise.
- **Promote environmental sustainability:** Be mindful of the environmental impact of

your professional activities and seek opportunities to minimize your footprint.

- **Give back to your community:** Dedicate time and resources to causes you care about, whether it's volunteering your skills or financially supporting worthy organizations.

**Leading with purpose and embracing social responsibility are not merely add-ons to your vision; they are integral components.** By integrating these elements, you ensure your career journey makes a meaningful contribution to the world, leaving a lasting legacy that extends far beyond your professional achievements.

# APPENDIX A

# OTHER BOOKS BY THE SAME AUTHOR

1. The Perfect Launch-out
2. High-performance Checklist
3. Life Success System
4. Positioning for Quality Life
5. Health Intelligence
6. Everything is all about Selling

All books by Lillian Oyeleye are available on Amazon.com and Selar.co . Simply search any of these titles from the same store where you bought this book. You can also visit our website by clicking Medlicos .

# APPENDIX B

# CONNECT WITH US

For feedback, send us an Email. We would love to hear from you

Don't be left behind, join our community on Telegram and WhatsApp.

**Email** - contact.medlicos@gmail.com

**Telegram** - https://t.me/IISMbyMedlicos

**WhatsApp** - https://chat.whatsapp.com/CpvQDtdCMWe0aYHjmqsA6F

# BECOME A BRILLIANT VISION EXECUTIVE

### Go Beyond the Spark

Is your career a lukewarm latte – offering a dull pick-me-up but failing to truly satisfy? Many professionals find themselves stuck in a cycle of uninspiring jobs, their potential simmering just below the surface. This book throws open the doors to a professional kitchen unlike any other – one where you craft the recipe for a fulfilling career journey.

Forget the pre-made options. Here, you'll discover the secret ingredients to ignite your vision, a powerful force that propels you towards a career rich in meaning, purpose, and impact.

This book serves as your essential culinary guide, equipping you with the tools and strategies to:

- **Uncover your purpose:** The underlying "why" that fuels your passion and shapes your career aspirations.
- **Spark your big idea:** The unique blend of skills, talents, and experiences that make your professional vision truly your own.
- **Craft your guiding vision:** A concise yet powerful statement that encapsulates your aspirations, values, and the impact you want to make.

"Become a Brilliant Vision Executive" is more than just a career guide; it's an invitation to a **professional awakening**. It's about igniting your passion, cultivating a supportive network, and mastering the skills to turn your vision into a reality that's as delicious as it is impactful.

### About the Author

**Lillian Oyeleye** is the Founder of Medlicos and the Chief Operating Officer (COO) at Cadamo Investment Ltd. She is a High-performance Coach on a mission to help individuals, achievers, and organizations transition from their current positions, to where they desire, deserve, and are designed to be.

She is a Pharmacist who obtained her B.pharm from Obafemi Awolowo University where she graduated with distinction. Also, she is certified in Global Mental Health by the University of Washington, Seattle.

Lillian has authored several books on personal development, transformation, growth, sales and health. She impacts many through her podcast called 'High-performance with Lillian, courses, as well as her signature program called Medlicos High-performance Academy (MHA).

Beyond her career, She is a kingdom woman, who is passionate about the message of Christ. She is the convener of The She Believes (TSB), the female arm of Engaging the Truth Team (ETT) Ministry and the host of a talk show called ETT Explore.

**Published by:**

Prestige Editors

www.ingramcontent.com/pod-product-compliance
Lightning Source LLC
Chambersburg PA
CBHW070952220526
45471CB00007B/2996